Hodder Cambridge Primary

English

Learner's Book
Stage 1

Sarah Snashall
Series Editor: Dr Wendy Jolliffe

HODDER
EDUCATION
AN HACHETTE UK COMPANY

The Publishers would like to thank the following for permission to reproduce copyright material:

Acknowledgements
p4–5, p52 used by permission of Sarah Snashall; p12–13, *Lily and the Blue Kangaroo at the Zoo* poem and illustrations © Emma Chichester Clark from *With Love: A Celebration of Words and Pictures for the Very Young*, 2004 (Orchard Books); p16, from *Five Minutes' Peace* by Jill Murphy ©1986 Jill Murphy reproduced by permission Walker Books Ltd, London SE11 5HJ *www.walker.co.uk*; p86 *Ice Cream Cone* by Heidi E.Y. Stemple, copyright © 1997 by Heidi E.Y. Stemple, reprinted by permission of Curtis Brown, Ltd; p90, *Happy* by Michaela Morgan © Michaela Morgan reproduced by permission of the author; p94, *Sampan* by Tao Lang Pee from *Can I Buy a Slice of Sky?: Poems from Black, Asian and American Indian Cultures* published by Hodder Education; p98, illustration from *All Change* written by Ian Whybrow, illustrated by David Melling and published by Hodder; p100, from *The Tiger Who Came to Tea* by Judith Kerr and published by HarperCollins; p106, from *The Way Back Home* by Oliver Jeffers and published by HarperCollins; p132, from *Rumble in the Jungle* by Giles Andreae published by Orchard Books; p136, *Mice* by Rose Fyleman, reprinted by permission of The Society of Authors as the Literary Representative of the Estate of Rose Fyleman; p140, *Snake in School* by Debjani Chatterjee from *A Dragon in the Classroom and other Poems about School*, compiled by Brian Moses, Wayland 2010, illustration by Kelly Waldek.

Every effort has been made to trace all copyright holders, but if any have been inadvertently overlooked the Publishers will be pleased to make the necessary arrangements at the first opportunity.

Although every effort has been made to ensure that website addresses are correct at time of going to press, Hodder Education cannot be held responsible for the content of any website mentioned in this book. It is sometimes possible to find a relocated web page by typing in the address of the home page for a website in the URL window of your browser.

Hachette UK's policy is to use papers that are natural, renewable and recyclable products and made from wood grown in sustainable forests. The logging and manufacturing processes are expected to conform to the environmental regulations of the country of origin.

Orders: please contact Bookpoint Ltd, 130 Milton Park, Abingdon, Oxon OX14 4SB. Telephone: +44 (0)1235 827720. Fax: +44 (0)1235 400454. Lines are open 9.00a.m.–5.00p.m., Monday to Saturday, with a 24-hour message answering service. Visit our website at www.hoddereducation.com

© Sarah Snashall 2015
First published in 2015 by
Hodder Education,
An Hachette UK Company
Carmelite House
50 Victoria Embankment
London EC4Y 0DZ

Impression number   10 9 8 7
Year   2019 2018

Cover illustration by Sandy Lightley
Illustrations by Marleen Visser
Typeset in Swissforall in 17pt by Resolution
Printed in Italy

A catalogue record for this title is available from the British Library

ISBN 978 1471 831003

Contents

Stories about my world

I know one word on the page means one spoken word.

Helpful hints

Follow the words from left to right.

The dragon in the hall

Sonja woke up.

She was thirsty but there was a monster under her bed, spiders in her slippers and a dragon in the hall.

The baby began to cry.

Sonja got out of bed. She forgot about the monster. She put on her slippers. She forgot about the spiders.

1 Listen to your teacher reading the story. Point to each word in turn as your teacher reads.

I know to read from left to right.

She ran across the hall. She forgot about the dragon. She stroked the baby's back. "Shush. I'm here."

Sonja's mother came into the room. "Thank you, darling. You are a good sister. What about the monster, the spiders and the dragon?"

"Don't be silly, Mummy," said Sonja. "There aren't any!"

By Sarah Snashall

Starting phonemes

I can hear the phonemes at the beginning of words.

1 What phoneme do these words start with? Write the letter.
Try to write the word.

Helpful hints

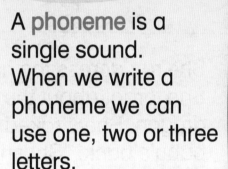

A phoneme is a single sound. When we write a phoneme we can use one, two or three letters.
These words have three phonemes:
- cat – c-a-t
- bath – b-a-th
- check – ch-e-ck

2 Which words start with the same phoneme?

nip   pin   leg   map

pip   lot   nut   mum

3 Find a word in the story on pages 4 and 5 that starts with these phonemes:

b   h   r

Sh

I know that sh is one phoneme.

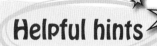

Helpful hints

These letters make a new phoneme when put together:
sh
Do the action and say the sound.
Read these words:
- shop
- wish

1 Point to the objects that start with a sh phoneme.
Point to the objects that start with an s phoneme.

2 a Write two words from the story on pages 4 and 5 that start with the sh phoneme.
b Write two words from the story that start with the s phoneme.

Beginning, middle and end

I can talk about the beginning, middle and end of a story.

Helpful hints

We use these words to talk about a story:
Beginning: the start of a story where we find out who is in the story and where they are.
Middle: the main part of the story.
End: the last part of a story.

1 Write 'Beginning', 'Middle' or 'End' for these parts of the story on pages 4 and 5.
  a Sonja tells her mother that there are no monsters.
  b Sonja is in bed.
  c Sonja comforts the baby when she cries.

2 Write 'true' or 'false':
  a There is a monster under Sonja's bed.
  b Sonja is brave in the story.
  c Sonja is a good sister.
  d Sonja fights the dragon.

Talk Partners

Tell your partner about a time when you were scared. Why were you scared? What did you do?

I can spell short words.

Writing **sh** and **ch**

Helpful hints

ch
Do the action and say the sound.
Read these words:
- chop
- chip

Writing presentation
Practise writing **sh** and **ch**.

sh   sh   sh   sh
ch   ch   ch   ch

1 Write these words. Each one has **sh** or **ch** in it.

a   _ _ ick

b   fi _ _

c   _ _ ip

d   _ _ op

e   _ _ in

Sentences

I pause at the end of sentences.

I can recognise a sentence.

Helpful hints

A **sentence** has a capital letter at the beginning and a full stop at the end.
The shark ate my hat.

When we read a story, we pause for a moment between sentences.

1

Read this story.
Count the sentences.

Sonja was sad in bed.
She had lost her bunny.
Mum came. Here's bunny.

2

Which of these are sentences?
a Please come to my party.
b the fast car
c Mrs Brown
d I am playing with my toys.

I know that sentences start with a capital letter.

I can use a full stop.

More sentences

Talk Partners

Read the story on page 10 out loud to a partner. Ask them to tell you if you paused between sentences. Listen to your partner reading the story.

1 These sentences are missing something. Write them out correctly.

a   my mum has a green dress
b   I have lost my book
c   the ball has gone over the wall
d   the children will help

Try this

Look at these pictures.
Finish these sentences.

a   There is _____.

b   The shop _____.

Lily and Blue Kangaroo at the Zoo

I can use phonics to read words I don't know.

Lily and Blue Kangaroo spent the day with their friends at the zoo.

The monkeys were naughty the lions were **haughty**,

How do you do?

Did you know?

There are many stories about Lily and Blue Kangaroo to read. Blue Kangaroo often gets lost!

but a parrot said, "How do you do?"

Helpful hints

Use phonics to read words you don't know. Look for letter patterns you know. Put them together to read the word: h-u-ll-a-b-a-l-oo

Glossary

haughty (h-or-t-ee): proud
hullabaloo: a big fuss

When Lily lost Blue Kangaroo she caused a great **hullabaloo**!

Everyone hurried, they needn't have worried ...

... he popped up and said,

"Peekaboo!"

By Emma Chichester Clark

Lost at the zoo

I can read some words on sight.

1

Find these words in the story on pages 12–13.
Practise reading and writing them.

> were   said   they   she
> have   you   do

2

What happens in the story? Choose an answer.

a Who gets lost at the zoo?

Lily   Blue Kangaroo

b Who says, "How do you do?"

a parrot   a monkey

c Which animal is naughty?

the lions   the monkeys

d Where is Blue Kangaroo?

with the kangaroos   with the zoo keeper

Feelings

When I read a story, I can think of something that has happened to me.

1 How does Lily feel in the story? Choose a word:

worried   happy

a When Lily loses Blue Kangaroo she feels _____.

b When Lily finds Blue Kangaroo she feels _____.

Talk Partners

Tell your partner about a time when you lost something. How did you feel? Talk clearly so that your partner can hear. Listen to what happened to him or her. Look at him or her when they talk.

2 Draw some pictures showing what happened to you. Write a sentence to go with your pictures, for example:

I lost my _____ when _____.

When I lost my _____ I felt _____.

Five Minutes' Peace

I can read along with a story.

The children were having breakfast. This was not a pleasant sight.

Mrs Large took a tray from the cupboard. She set it with a teapot, a milk jug, her favourite cup and saucer, a plate of marmalade toast and a leftover cake from yesterday. She stuffed the morning paper into her pocket and sneaked off towards the door.

1 Listen to your teacher read the story. Follow with your finger. Join in when your teacher reads it again.

I can say what
might happen next.

"Where are you going with that tray, Mum?" asked Laura.
"To the bathroom," said Mrs Large.
"Why?" asked the other two children.
"Because I want five minutes' peace from *you* lot," said
Mrs Large. "That's why."

"Can we come?"
asked Lester as they
trailed up the stairs
behind her.
"No," said Mrs Large,
"you can't."

By Jill Murphy

2 What do you think will happen next in the story?

I can talk about what happens in a story.

Who and where

Helpful hints

Characters – the people or animals in the story.
Setting – where the story takes place.
There can be lots of characters and settings in a story.

1 Answer these questions using these pictures to help you.

a Who are the characters in the story on pages 16–17?
b Where is the story set (the setting)?
c What are the children doing in the kitchen?
d Where is Mrs Large going?
e What does Mrs Large want?

Talk Partners

The children do join Mrs Large in the bathroom. Look at this picture of Mrs Large. How does she feel? How do the children feel?

Retelling a story

I can retell a story.

1 Use this story map to tell the story of *Five Minutes' Peace* to a friend. Remember to talk clearly.

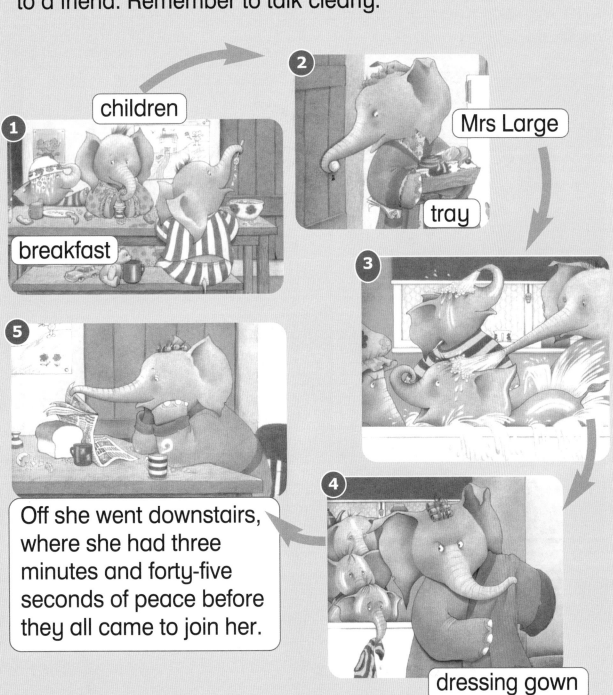

children

2 Mrs Large

1 breakfast

tray

3

5

Off she went downstairs, where she had three minutes and forty-five seconds of peace before they all came to join her.

4

dressing gown

Peace and quiet

I look at people to show I'm listening.

1 Use these pictures to tell yourself a story about a boy who wants some peace. Draw some pictures to tell your own story.

Talk Partners

Tell your story to a friend. Listen to their story. Remember to look at your friend when he or she talks.

I can write simple captions.

I can write a sentence.

Writing captions

Helpful hints

- When you don't know how to spell a word, sound out the phonemes in turn.
- A **caption** is a sentence that tells you about a picture or photograph.

1 Write a sentence or just some words as a caption for each picture you have drawn for page 20. Use the checklist below to check your work.

Peace at last.

What have I learnt?

I have:
- used a capital letter at the start of a sentence
- used a full stop at the end of a sentence
- used a capital letter for names
- spelt the words I know correctly
- used phonics to spell words I don't know.

Unit 2 Signs, labels and instructions

Signs

1 Read these signs. What are they telling you to do?

2 Look for signs around your classroom.

Helpful hints

Instructions tell us to do something:
- Take care.
- Sit down.

They can tell us not to do something:
- Don't run.
- Don't talk.

Push

Don't tap the glass

Talk to me

Stroke me

Don't feed me

Take care: I bite

Bossy words

I can use command words.

Helpful hints

Instructions use command words.
These are bossy words.
- **Jump** up and down.
- **Find** your hat.
- Don't **sit** here.

1 Find these bossy words in the pet shop signs on pages 22–23:

take   feed   talk   stroke   shout
run   pay   tap   push

2 Write the bossy words.
a Pop the balloon.
b Cut the cake.
c Put on your coat.
d Sit down.
e Try hard.

Role play

I can take part in a role play.

Talk Partners

In pairs, play pet shops.
- Learner 1: Go into the shop. Choose a pet.
- Learner 2: You are the shopkeeper. Say how to look after the pet.

Talk clearly so your partner can hear you.

1 Choose a bossy word to go with each of these pictures:

jump   hop   kick   run

a    b    c    d

What are they saying?

Come up! Play with me.
Find me.

Try this

Fiction or non-fiction?

I know that some texts look different.

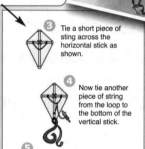

How to make a kite

⭐ **Helpful hints** ⭐

Instructions can tell you *how* to do something. For example:
* How to make a kite.
* How to look after your pet fish.

Instruction books look different from storybooks.

lists

pictures or photos

numbers

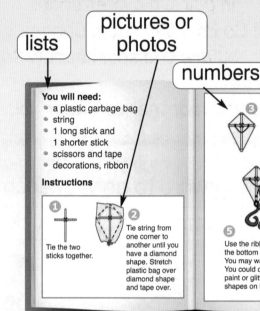

You will need:
* a plastic garbage bag
* string
* 1 long stick and 1 shorter stick
* scissors and tape
* decorations, ribbon

Instructions

① Tie the two sticks together.

② Tie string from one corner to another until you have a diamond shape. Stretch plastic bag over diamond shape and tape over.

③ Tie a short piece of sting across the horizontal stick as shown.

④ Now tie another piece of string from the loop to the bottom of the vertical stick.

⑤ Use the ribbon and tie a tail onto the bottom corner. You may want to add bows. You could decorate your kite with paint or glitter and stick coloured shapes on it.

Talk Partners

Look at a recipe book with a friend. Look at a storybook with a friend. Tell each other how are they different.

1 Write an instruction word:

a c _ _

b p _ sh

c _ u ll

d s t _ _ _

Reading and writing th

I can read words with **ch**, **th** and **sh**.

Helpful hints

1

Write the words with **th**.
Underline **th**.

thing   wish   chip   path
ten   maths   time   teeth
sheet   cloth

th
Say the sound.
Read these words:
- thin
- thick
- bath
- moth

thumb

2

Complete the captions and match them to the pictures.

a   fi_ _ for lun_ _

b   _ _ ip at sea

c   too_ _ bru _ _ and clo_ _

1

2

3

Reading instructions

I can read short words.

How to make chocolate fruit kebabs

You will need

6 grapes
1 apple
1 banana
1 mango
1 bar of chocolate
wooden skewers

What to do

1 Peel the fruit and cut it up.

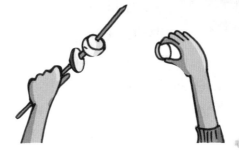

2 Put the fruit on the skewers.

3 Now melt the chocolate.

4 Pour the chocolate on to the kebabs.

5 When cool – eat!

In the right order

I know that some texts look different.

Talk Partners

Read the instructions on pages 28–29 with a partner. Point to:

a the first thing you must do
b the list of things you need
c a picture of the last thing you must do.

Helpful hints

We follow instructions in order. We must do the things we are told to do in the right order or the instructions will not work.

1 Put these in order.
a Go outside.
b Put on socks.
c Put on shoes.

2 Match the caption below to each picture.
a Cut up fruit.
b Melt chocolate.
c Eat.

Words

I can read some words on sight.

1 Learn these words:

> the   with   when   this
> now   there   up

a Write two words from the cloud above that start with the **w** phoneme.

b Find three words that start with the **th** phoneme.

c Find two words with the **i** phoneme.

2 Choose a word from the cloud above for each sentence.

a _____ put on a hat.

b Take _____ apple.

c Go _____ there.

d Sit _____ me.

Using and

I can use the word **and**.

1 Find **and** in *How to make chocolate fruit kebabs* on page 29.

How to make chocolate fruit kebabs on page 29.

Helpful hints

We use the word **and** to say two things in a sentence.

2 Find **and** in these sentences:

a Get off the bus and go to the shop.
b Take the coat and bag from the peg.
c See the duck and frog on the pond.
d Please get the bat and ball.

3 Finish these sentences. Choose an ending from the cloud.

and goats.   and listen.   and paper.   and eat your fruit.

a Find the pens _____
b Wash your hands _____
c Feed the sheep _____
d Sit on the rug _____

Writing words and sentences

I can form letters correctly.

1 Read these sentences.
Put them together with **and**.
The first one has been done for you.

a Take your bag. Take your hat.
Take your bag and hat.

b I like apples. I like bananas.

c The ball is big. The ball is red.

d Shut the door. Sit down.

Writing presentation

Practise writing **th.**

t h   t h   t h   t h

Write these words.

the   this   there   with

I can sound out words I don't know.

How to *do a forward roll*

What you need:
- a large flat area
- sports clothes.

1 Stand up in a large flat area.

2 Bend your knees.

3 Bend your elbows and put your hands on the ground.

4 Drop your head and tuck in your chin.

5 Quickly push off and roll over on to your back and then to your feet.

6 Stand up.

Giving instructions

I can listen to instructions.

1 Find these things in *How to do a forward roll* on pages 34–35.
  a These bossy words: stand up, bend, push, roll.
  b A list of what you need.
  c Point number 4.
  d The picture of the person rolling.

2 Choose the correct bossy words to finish the sentences:

  a _____ up.

Stand	The boy stands

  b _____ over quickly.

Roll	She rolls

  c _____ your legs.

Bend	You bend

Talk Partners   Make up a pattern of jumps, skips and runs. Teach your partner. Can they follow your instructions? Swap roles. Can you follow what they tell you to do?

Two letters – one sound

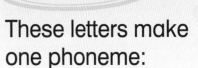

I can hear phonemes in words. I know that **sh**, **ch** and **th** are one sound.

1 Write the words that have two letters making one phoneme. Draw a line underneath the letters making the phoneme.

sack	puff	fog	chum
off	leg	less	bell
doll	cat	sun	rocket
dull	of	sell	set
mess	fuss		shock

Helpful hints

These letters make one phoneme:
- **sh** as in **sh**in
- **th** as in **th**in
- **ch** as in **ch**in
- **ff** as in hu**ff**
- **ll** as in hi**ll**
- **ss** as in hi**ss**
- **ck** as in so**ck**

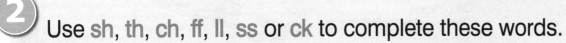

2 Use **sh**, **th**, **ch**, **ff**, **ll**, **ss** or **ck** to complete these words.

a hi__

e __eep

b hi__

f mo__

c cli__

g __illy

d ki__

How to make a butterfly

Talk Partners

Look at these pictures with a partner.
Talk about how to make a wooden spoon butterfly.

I can create some instruction sentences.

I can write a sentence.

I can write an instruction.

1 Make the butterfly from page 38.

a First, draw a picture of each stage.

b Show your pictures to a friend and tell them how to make the butterfly.

c Write some words to tell someone else how to make it. Use these words to help you:

> spoon   paint   glue   pipe cleaners   paper
> cut out   stick on   paint a pattern

What have I learnt?

Use this list to check your instructions. I have:
- used phonics to spell words
- used a full stop at the end of a sentence
- used a capital letter at the start of a sentence
- used **and**.

Did you know that butterflies taste with their feet!

Unit 3 Simple rhymes

Round and round the mango tree

Round and round the mango tree
Who did run but little me,
With ten bananas in my pail
And ten red monkeys at my tail!

By Uzo Unobagha

I can join in with a poem.

Action rhymes

I can recite a poem.

Talk Partners

Read 'Round and round the mango tree' with a partner. Try to learn it by heart.

1 Match the number to the word. Point to the number and the word that match for each.

five   5
one   3
four   1
three   4   2
two

2 Pair up words in the cloud that rhyme.

pail   me   tail   tree

Write short words

I can write short words.

1 Read the words in the cloud:

then   let   did   this

Change the words:
a **then** – change the first phoneme to t.
What word do you get?
b **did** – change the last phoneme to p.
What word do you get?
c **let** – change the last phoneme to g.
What word do you get?
d **this** – change the first phoneme to h.
What word do you get?
e **then** – change the middle phoneme to a.
What word do you get?

2 Write the word.

Holding a pencil

I can hold my pencil well.

1 Find these words in the poem on page 40.

who   tree   ten   my   little

a Which word rhymes with **boo**?
b Which word starts with the **h** phoneme?
c Which word rhymes with **hi**?

Writing presentation

Practise writing these words:

who who who who
tree tree tree tree
ten ten ten ten
my my my my
little little little little

Helpful hints

Hold your pencil like this.

I can recite a poem.

Row, row, row your boat

Row, row, row your boat
Gently down the stream.
Merrily, merrily, merrily, merrily,
Life is but a dream.

Row, row, row your boat
Gently down the stream.
If you see a crocodile
Don't forget to scream.

(SCREAM)

Row, row, row your boat
Gently to the shore.
If you see a lion there
Don't forget to roar.

(ROAR)

1 Listen to your teacher read this poem.
Learn this poem by heart.

Answering questions

I can answer questions.

1 Answer these questions with your partner.
Say the answers clearly.

a Where is the person in the poem?
  How do you know?
b Is he or she happy? Yes or no?
  How do you know?
c What water animal are they looking for?
  Will they be pleased if they see it?
d What will they do if they see a lion?

Talk Partners

Talk to your partner about the poem. Listen to their answers. Ask them:

a Would you rather see a tiger, a mouse or an elephant? Why?
b Would you rather see a lion or a crocodile? Why?
c Would you rather fall out of the boat or forget your sandwiches?
d Which of these boats would you prefer:

e Ask your own questions.

Patterns in poems

> I can talk about the words in a poem.

1 Count the times you can see these words in the poem on page 44.
  a Row, row, row your boat
  b Gently down the stream
  c Merrily
  d If you see

2 Match the words that rhyme:

beach

squeak

river

creek

shiver

screech

My rhyme

I can make up my own rhyme.

1 Use words from activity 2 on page 46 to complete these verses:

Row, row, row your boat
Gently to the _____.
If you see a shark there
Don't forget to _____.

Row, row, row your boat
Gently down the _____.
If you see a polar bear
Don't forget to _____.

Row, row, row your boat
Gently down the _____.
If you see a little mouse
Don't forget to _____.

I am the music man

I am the music man
I come from down your way
And I can play ...
What can you play?

I can play the piano
pi-a pi-a piano piano piano
pi-a pi-a piano pi-a piano.

I am the music man
I come from down your way
And I can play ...
What can you play?

I can play the big bass drum
Om-pa om-pa om-pa-pa, om-pa-pa, om-pa-pa
Om-pa om-pa om-pa-pa, om-pa, om-pa-pa.

Did you know?

The world's largest drum is nearly six metres tall. It is in South Korea.

I know that capital
I is used for I.

1 Find lines that are the same in the poem on page 48.

2 Enjoy the poem.
a Learn the poem by heart.
b Make up and say your own verses with these instruments. Make up your own noises.

> I can play the _____ (trombone/violin/triangle).

c Make up some actions.

3 Write these sentences with capital letters.
a may i come?
b i will go.
c here i am.

Helpful hints

We always write I with a capital letter.

What have I learnt?

Check your new verse. I have:
- used a capital letter for I
- used phonics to write the sound of the instrument
- used lines from the 'Music man' poem
- added some actions.

QUIZ 1

1 Put this story in order. Write 'Beginning', 'Middle' or 'End'.

  a We sat on the sand. We had an ice cream.

  b We went home.

  c Mum and I went to the seaside.

2 Write **sh**, **th** or **ch** to finish the words:

  a wi __    **b** tee __

  c __ op    **d** wa __

  e pa __

3 Use these words to write a sentence. Remember to use full stops and a capital letter.

  a girl the has of pop can a

  b hot the is pot

  c to will i top get the

  d the and Jon i to shop hop

4 Use **and** to make one sentence.
   a The fox is big. The fox is red.
   b I have a fish in my net. I have a shell in my net.
   c I like to hop. I like to jump.
   d The boy has a book. The boy has a pen.

5 Write a caption for the pictures.

a

sun

man

ran

The _____

b

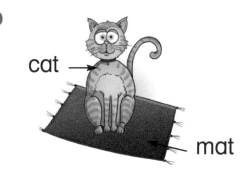

cat

mat

The _____

c

car

traffic jam

The _____

d

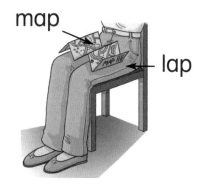

map

lap

The _____

6 Match the words that rhyme.

shell   net   pot   hop

   shop   not   vet   fell

Traditional stories

I can suggest what might happen next.

The lion and the mouse

Once upon a time, a lion was sleeping in the sun. As he slept, a little mouse ran on to the lion's nose and woke him up. The lion picked up the mouse by its tail and opened his sleepy mouth to eat it.

"Stop!" said the mouse. "Do not eat me. I might be able to help you one day."

The lion thought this very funny. "I will let you go, brave little mouse," he said with a grin, "But I don't think you can ever help me."

Talk Partners

Ask your partner: What do you think will happen next? Can a mouse help a lion?

I can read along with a story.

The mouse ran off and the lion went back to sleep. But as he slept hunters came and tied him up. The lion woke and roared. The little mouse heard and came running.

At once the mouse started to nibble away at the ropes. When the lion was free he bowed to the little mouse.

"Thank you, great mouse, for saving my life and teaching me a lesson."

By Aesop, retold by Sarah Snashall

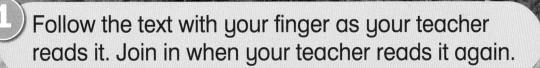

1 Follow the text with your finger as your teacher reads it. Join in when your teacher reads it again.

br, sl and gr

I can read blends.

1 Find these words in the story on pages 52–53. Write them down. Draw a line under the first two letters.

- brave
- grin
- great
- sleeping
- slept

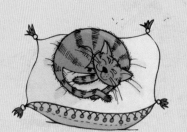

2 Choose **br**, **gr** or **sl** to complete the word:

a __ ing

b __ ush

c __ ab

d __ een

e __ ass

f __ip

g __ eep

Sight words

I can read some words on sight.

Helpful hints ⭐

Read these words:

him	his	came
went	off	don't
	help	

- Practise reading them quickly.
- Find the words in the story on pages 52–53.

1 Use the words in the sentences:

don't   help   went   his

a Please give Ravi _____ hat.
b The man _____ home.
c Please _____ jump off the wall.
d Do you need him to _____ you?

2 Look at the words in the Helpul hints box again.
Guess the word:
a Which word means **do not**? d _ _ ' _?
b Which word has a **z** phoneme spelt **s**? h _ _
c Which word has two letters making one phoneme? o _ _
d Which word has the blend **nt**? w _ _ _

Act it out

I can take part in a role play.

Talk Partners

How do the characters feel? Talk to your partner.

a   When the lion catches the mouse, the mouse feels:
    happy   scared   bored

b   When the mouse talks to the lion, the lion feels:
    amused   cross   tired

c   When the hunters tie up the lion, the lion feels:
    happy   scared   bored

1 You are going to act out *The lion and the mouse* with a group.
You will need to decide who will be:

- the mouse
- the lion
- the two hunters.

Make masks.

2 Think of something for the characters to say.

I can write sentences to retell a story.

Pictures

1 Draw pictures to tell the story of *The lion and the mouse.*
Write a sentence for each picture.

Practise telling the whole story with two friends.

Try this

a Choose two pictures each and practise telling that part of the story.

b Make up some actions to go with your part.

c What will your characters say?

d Start: 'Once upon a time …'

e Practise many times then tell your story together.

The enormous turnip

1. Once upon a time there was a turnip farmer and his wife. Mr and Mrs Root planted turnip seeds in a neat line. The sun shone and the rain fell, and the turnip seeds grew and grew.

2. In time, Mr and Mrs Root pulled up the turnips: one, two, three, four, five, six, seven, eight, nine ...

3. ... but the last turnip was really enormous. They pulled and they heaved, and they heaved and they pulled, but they could not pull it up.

4. The donkey came to help. It pulled Mr Root, Mr Root pulled Mrs Root and Mrs Root pulled the turnip. They pulled and they heaved, but they could not pull up the turnip.

5. The sheep and the chicken came to help. They pulled the donkey, the donkey pulled Mr Root, Mr Root pulled Mrs Root and Mrs Root pulled the turnip. They pulled and they heaved, but they could not pull up the turnip.

6. A little mouse came to help. It pulled the chicken, the chicken pulled the sheep, the sheep pulled the donkey, the donkey pulled Mr Root, Mr Root pulled Mrs Root and Mrs Root pulled the turnip. They pulled and they heaved when ... POP – out came the enormous turnip.

7. Mrs Root fell on Mr Root, Mr Root fell on the donkey, the donkey fell on the sheep, the sheep fell on the chicken and the chicken fell on the ground because the little mouse had scampered away to safety.

By Alexei Tolstoy, retold by Sarah Snashall

Beginning, middle and end

I can talk about the beginning, middle and end.

1 Order these sentences. Write: beginning, middle or end.
a The turnip came out – POP!
b Mr and Mrs Root planted seeds.
c They tried to pull up the turnip.

2 Answer these questions about *The enormous turnip*.
a Who are the main characters?
b What do they want to do?
c Who is the last character to help?
d How many characters help pull up the turnip?

Talk Partners

What do you learn from this story?

a Mice are stronger than people.

or

b It's good to work together.

Story words

I can talk about the words in a story.

Helpful hints

Stories often start in one of these ways:
- Once upon a time
- There once was
- One day

Traditional stories sometimes have lines that are repeated. For example, *they pulled and they heaved.*

1 How many times can you find these words in the story on pages 58–59?
a Once upon a time
b they pulled and they heaved
c Mr Root pulled Mrs Root and Mrs Root pulled the turnip
d came to help

2 Choose a story starter for each story below.

There once was   Once upon a time
One day

a _____ there was a girl called Cinderella.
b _____ a giant who lived on a hill.
c _____ Tom found a gold egg.

Retelling a story

I can retell a story.

Talk Partners

Use these pictures to retell *The enormous turnip.*
Use these words:

a Once upon a time
b but she could not pull up the turnip.

Mr and Mrs Root

heaved

turnip

donkey sheep chicken mouse

Story language

I can use story language.

1 **What do these characters say?**

a

b

2 Draw four pictures for *The enormous turnip.*
Write a sentence under each to tell the story.
  a Start 'Once upon a time'.
  b Use 'they heaved and they pulled' twice.
  c Add one of the lines from activity 1.
  d Use a capital letter and a full stop for each sentence.

I can pause at the end of sentences.

The paintbrush

Once upon a time, there was a kind boy call Ma Liang who loved to draw. One night as he slept, he had a dream about a paintbrush. Everything the brush painted became real. In the morning he found the paintbrush on the floor by his bed.

Ma Liang used the paintbrush to draw food and water for anyone who needed it.

But in the village there lived a mean, rich man. He captured Ma Liang and said, "Draw gold for me and I will set you free."

 Listen to your teacher read the story two times. Then read the story aloud. Pause at the end of each sentence.

I can talk about what happens in a story.

Ma Liang drew a golden island far out to sea and a ship on the shore. The rich man jumped into the ship and set off for the island. When the ship was far from land, Ma Liang drew a large wave that sank the ship. The rich man was never seen again.

Everyone in the village was happy and Ma Liang and his paintbrush were loved by everyone.

A traditional Chinese story retold by Sarah Snashall

Talk Partners

Tell your partner what happens in the story. Ask you partner to help you remember things you may have forgotten.

Using **and**

I can use the word **and**.

1 Answer these questions about the story on pages 64–65.
  a Who are the two main characters?
  b What did Ma Liang love to do?
  c How does Ma Liang feel when he finds the paintbrush?
  d Why does the rich man capture Ma Liang?
  e What happens to the rich man?

2 Use **and** to join these two sentences.
  a The day was hot. The day was sunny.
  b I have one book. I have one pen.
  c I will have a wash. I will go to bed.
  d He went to help Tom. He went to help Tim.
  e The mouse was brave. The mouse was clever.

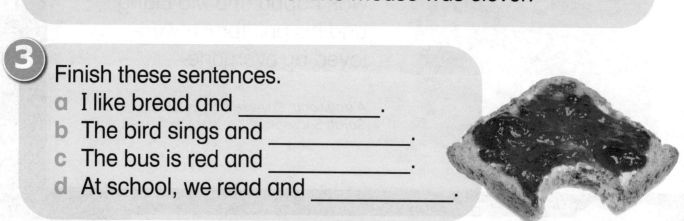

3 Finish these sentences.
  a I like bread and _____.
  b The bird sings and _____.
  c The bus is red and _____.
  d At school, we read and _____.

More blends

I can form my letters correctly.

1 In the story on pages 64–65, find:
a one word starting with **sl**
b one word starting with **fl**
c one word starting with **br**.

2 Practise writing these blends.

sl   sl   sl   sl   sl

fl   fl   fl   fl   fl

br   br   br   br   br

3 Practise writing these words.

draw   draw   draw   draw

sleep   sleep   sleep   sleep

floor   floor   floor   floor

brush   brush   brush   brush

Writing a sentence

I can use a full stop.

Talk Partners

Look at these pictures with a partner.
Say a short sentence for each one.

a

b

c

d

1. Write down your sentences. Remember to use a capital letter at the start of each sentence. Remember to use a full stop at the end of each sentence.

I can write a simple storybook.

Making a book

1 Make a mini-book like this. Draw pictures for the story and write your sentences.

a Fold a piece of paper and cut along the fold line shown in red.

b Fold the paper to make a mini-book.

 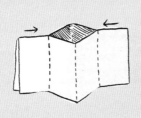 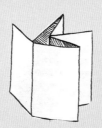

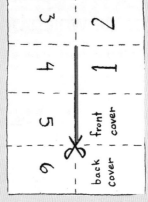

c Write the title. Write your name.

The Paintbrush

By A Nother

d Write the story.

Ma Liang found a paintbrush.

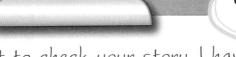

What have I learnt?

Use this checklist to check your story. I have:
- used phonics to spell words
- started every sentence with a capital letter
- finished every sentence with a full stop
- told the whole story of *The paintbrush*.

Unit 5 Reports and dictionaries

Different books

I know the parts of a book.

1 Decide which books are fiction or non-fiction?

a   b   c   d

Pirate Adventure

BIG Cats

Rivers

Alice in Wonderland

Helpful hints

Fiction and non-fiction books
- Fiction books tell us stories.
- Non-fiction books tell us facts.

Helpful hints

The **contents** page tells you where to find information in the book.

Contents

Big cats   4
Lions   6
Tigers   8
Cheetahs   10
Leopards   12
Baby cats   14

Report books are books that tell us about something.

A **heading** tells you what the words below will be about.

Tigers
Tigers are the biggest cats. They live in forests in Asia.

People try to help tigers.

In trouble
There are not many tigers left.

Tigers have striped coats to help them hide in the shadows.

A **caption** tells you about a picture.

Report books

I can talk about the books I like.

BIG Cats

Rivers

1 Look inside a report book.
  a Find:
   • a photograph
   • a caption
   • a heading.
  b What is the book about?

2 Find some books in your classroom.
  a Sort them into fiction and non-fiction.
  b Sort them into 'Books I want to read' and 'Books I don't want to read'. Show your books to a friend.

3 Match the photograph to the caption.

a

b

c

   • Lions sleep in the day.
   • Tigers have stripes.
   • Baby cats like to play.

Lego

Do you have any Lego?
With Lego bricks you can
make anything you want.

Wooden toys
The first Lego toys were
made of wood.

*Lego made a wooden duck
and wooden building blocks.*

The plastic brick
Now Lego make
plastic bricks and
mini-figures.

*There are Lego kits to
go with famous movies.*

I can read aloud on my own.

Legoland
There are Lego theme parks all over the world.

Legoland has rides and amazing Lego models.

Largest model
The biggest Lego model is a life-size Star Wars plane.

This spaceship used five million bricks.

1 Follow the text as your teacher reads it two times. Then try to read it aloud yourself.

Who, what, where or when?

Talk Partners

Say which of these statements is 'true' or 'false'.

a Lego made wooden toys.
b You can only make planes with Lego.
c The biggest Lego model was a duck.
d There are rides at Legoland.

Helpful hints

Reports can tell us:
- who
- what
- where
- when.

1 Can you find these things in the text on page 73?
a photograph
b caption
c heading

 I can use phonics to write words.

 I can write a simple sentence.

My favourite toy

1 Draw a picture of your favourite toy.
  a Write its name at the top.
  b Write two words about the toy.

Talk Partners Share your picture with a partner.

Tell them:
  • who gave you the toy
  • when you use it or play with it
  • what you do with it.

2 Write a sentence about your toy.
For example: *My polar bear is white and fluffy.*
  a Say two things about your toy.
  b Use a capital letter.
  c Use **and** in your sentence.
  d Use a full stop.
  e Say each word slowly to yourself. Listen for each phoneme. Write the letters for the phoneme.

Try this

Write a second sentence about your toy.

Animals

I can use phonics to read words I don't know.

Talk Partners

Read this with a partner. Work out words you do not know together using phonics. Look out for words you know how to read.

Animal homes

Animals make different homes. Find out about some of them here.

Ant colony

Ants live underground. They make little rooms and tunnels. The ants take the dirt from the tunnels to the top. This makes a pile of earth called an ant hill.

Many ants live together.

Weaver bird nests

Weaver birds make very large nests with many rooms – 400 weaver birds can live in the same nest.

Weaver birds make their nest from dry grass.

I can read some words on sight.

Beaver lodges

Beavers live in lodges.
The beaver swims underwater
to get inside.

Beavers make their home out of trees and mud.

Polar bear dens

A mother polar bear makes
a den in the snow. She stays
there to have her babies.

A mother polar bear stays in the den for half a year.

Who lives where?

animal	name of home
ant	colony
bird	nest
beaver	lodge
polar bear	den

Finding information

I know the parts of a book.

1 Find a part of the text on pages 76–77 that interests you and read that.

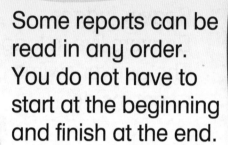

Helpful hints

Some reports can be read in any order. You do not have to start at the beginning and finish at the end.

Talk Partners

Point to the part of the text on pages 76–77 where you can find out about:

a polar bear homes
b ant homes
c large nests
d lodges.

Did you know?

The mother polar bear does not eat or drink for the six months she lives in the den.

2 Answer 'true' or 'false' to the following statements.

a Ants live in large groups.
b Weaver birds live alone.
c Weaver bird nests have lots of little rooms.
d Weavers go underwater to get in their homes.
e Father polar bears live in a den.

I can form my letters correctly.

I can find and spell some familiar words.

Tables

Helpful hints

Tables are a quick way to show lots of facts. Tables are made up of columns and rows.

Rows – these are lists that go along in a table.

Columns – these are the lists that go down in a table.

animal	name of home
ant	colony
bird	nest
beaver	lodge
polar bear	den

1
Use the table on page 77 to answer these questions:

a What is a bird's home called?
b Who lives in a lodge?
c Where do baby polar bears live?
d Who lives in a colony?

Writing presentation

Find these words in the text on pages 76–77. Practise writing them. Try to remember the spelling as you write them.

about   some   out   here   their   very   them

My favourite sport

1 Find out what sports your friends like. Write their answers in a table like this.

Name	Favourite sport or hobby	Second-favourite sport or hobby
Josh	*karate*	*drawing*
Mateo	*tennis*	*singing*
Pushkal	*football*	*cricket*

Talk Partners

Think about your favourite sport or hobby. Tell your partner:
- where you do it
- what you need to do it
- why you like it.

Ask your partner about their favourite sport or hobby. Listen to their answers. Ask more questions about it.

2 Write a report about your sport or hobby.
a Draw a picture of yourself doing your sport or hobby.
b Write a label for the things that you need, for example: football, karate suit, good voice.
c Write a sentence about why you like your hobby. Say it out loud first, then write it down.

Getting it right

I can read and talk about my own writing.

1 Show your report to a partner.
a   Tell them about the picture and read the labels and sentence to them.
b   Ask them to tell you how to make it better.
c   Ask them to help you with your spelling.
d   Look at their report and say something good about it and something that would make it even better.
e   Make your report better.

What have I learnt?

Check your report. I have:
- spelt words I know correctly
- tried to spell words I don't know
- used a capital letter and a full stop for my sentence
- put labels on my picture.

Fish to frog

I know that different texts look different.

F f

F

fish – an animal that lives underwater

flame – the orange part of a fire

flippers – the part of a swimming animal such as a penguin or a seal that flaps in the water and helps them swim

flower – the pretty part of a plant

football – a game where two teams try to kick a ball into a net

fork – a tool for eating

fox – a wild animal with red fur and a bushy tail

frog – an animal with smooth skin and webbed feet that lives near water

Talk Partners

Look at this page with a partner. How does it look different from a report? How does it look different from a story?

Dictionaries

I can read blends.

I can answer questions about a text.

★ Helpful hints ☆

A **dictionary** is a book that tells you what words mean.
The words in a dictionary are listed in the order of the alphabet.
- The **first words** start with the letter **a** and the **last words** start with the letter **z**.

1 Look at the dictionary text on page 82.
Answer these questions:
  a Which word is the orange part of a fire?
  b Which word comes after fox?
  c What is a frog?
  d Which word is a tool for eating?
  e What is a flower?

2 Practise these blends.
  a Find three words that start **fl** in the text on page 82.
  b Find one word starting with **fr** in the text.
  c Sort these words into three lists:
     words with **st**   words with **tr**   words with **sk**

     trick   ask   still   trim   skim   tusk   skill   trill
          lost   sty   stick   most   tree

Alphabetical order

I can put words in alphabetical order.

Helpful hints

Words that are listed in the order of the alphabet are said to be in **alphabetical order**.

These words are in alphabetical order:

- apple
- bat
- cake

1 Put these words in alphabetical order.
a brick, cup, ask
b egg, fish, did
c jug, gull, map

2 Get into a group with four friends. Use your names to line up in alphabetical order.

Try this

Put all the words from activity 1 into alphabetical order.

Dictionaries

I can answer questions.

1 Find these words in your dictionary. Race your partner to read the definition (what the word means) first.

foot   bird   leg

2 Draw a picture of:
a a drum
b a bag
c a hat.

Ask your partner to put the pictures in alphabetical order.

What have I learnt?

In this unit I have learnt:
- the difference between fiction and non-fiction books
- the different parts of a report book
- how to record information in a table
- to use clear handwriting
- to use a dictionary.

Playing with rhymes

Helpful hints

The letter **s** in sugar forms the phoneme **sh**.

Ice cream cone

Strawberry ice cream
cold and sweet;
sugar cone
my favourite treat!

Pink and sticky
melting drips;
I lick it off
my finger tips!

By Heidi E.Y. Stemple

Rhyming words

1 Find these blends in the poem on page 86.
  a Find words that start: **sw**, **tr**, **st**.
  b Find a word that ends: _ld.
  c Find a word with _lt_ in the middle.

2 Find these words in the poem on page 86.

sweet	treat	drips	tips

  a Underline the parts of the words that sound the same.
  b Underline the parts of the words that are spelt the same.

3 Match the words that rhyme. Underline the parts of the word that sound the same.

pump   bent   trips   went   slump
drips   dump   pips   sent

Playing with rhymes

I can learn and recite simple poems.

1 Answer questions about the poem on page 86.
  a Why does the ice cream drip?
  b Which flavour ice cream is it?
  c What happens to the person's fingers?
  d Why is the person happy?

Talk Partners

Read 'Ice cream cone' with your partner.
Imagine you are eating a sticky ice cream.

- Listen to the words that rhyme (sound the same).
- Read the poem out loud until you know it by heart.
- Perform the poem.

2 Answer these questions about the ice cream.
  a What does it look like?
  b What does it taste like?
  c What does it feel like?

Chocolate bar

I can write a new verse.

1 Use these lines to make up a poem about a chocolate bar.

> my chocolate bar
> in the sun
> has begun to run
> Sweet and sticky

2 Choose the words you would like to use to finish this poem about a lolly.

After school
I like to stop
and buy _____
(a sweet/a lolly/a book)
from the shop.

Lemon ice lolly
cold and _____ (tangy/juicy/sour)

it's so _____ (yummy/sticky/small)

I'll need _____ (a shower/another/a drink)

Writing presentation

Write your poem in your best handwriting.
Add a picture.

Happy

I'm as happy as a rainbow,
Or a dolphin in the sea.
As happy as a kangaroo,
Or a buzzy bee.
As happy as a flip-flop
Walking in the sand.
As happy as a big bass drum
in the happy band.

By Michaela Morgan

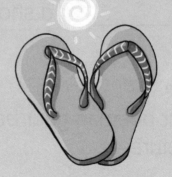

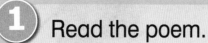

1 Read the poem.

I can talk about the words in a poem.

I can read many words on sight.

As happy as a ...

1 Answer questions about the poem on page 90.
a Which words are repeated in the poem?
b How many times are they repeated?
c Write down the six things that are happy.
d Which happy thing in the poem do you like best?
e Write down a happy thing that you would like to be.

2 Read these words with your partner. Listen to each phoneme. Hold up a finger for each phoneme.
a sand
b rainbow
c dolphin
d bee

Practise reading them a few times.

Talk Partners

Talk to your partner about how you can be 'as happy as a flip-flop'.

What a performance

Helpful hints

When we read a poem aloud to someone we should:
- look as if we like the poem
- look at the people we are reading to
- make our face match the poem (smile if it is a happy poem or look sad if it is a sad poem).

1 Read *Happy* on page 90 out loud.

a Practise the difficult words.
b Practise the whole poem.
c Read aloud in a clear voice.
d Look happy.
e Add some actions for:
- rainbow (make a rainbow shape with your arm)
- kangaroo (jump up and down)
- flip-flop (walk along)
- buzzy bee (make a **zz** sound)
- big bass drum (pretend to play a drum).

2 Listen to your classmates read the poem:
- look as if you are enjoying the poem
- smile at them
- look at them.

Having fun with words

I can spell many familiar words.

1 Make a list of all the things that make you happy.
Write down:
a something that you play (football, skipping)
b something you hear (a song, someone laughing)
c an animal you like
d a favourite food
e a favourite toy.

2 Use your list of happy things
to complete this poem:
As happy as _____
As happy as _____
As happy as _____
As happy as _____
As happy as _____
As happy as me!

Here is an example:

As happy as a winning goal
As happy as a baby's laugh
As happy as a tall giraffe
As happy as a pile of pancakes
As happy as a pile of books
As happy as me!

Helpful hints

Remember to spell the words you know correctly.
If you don't know how to spell a word:
• say the word slowly to hear each phoneme
• write the letters you know for each phoneme.

Sampan

Waves lap lap
Fish fins clap clap
Brown sails flap flap
Chop-sticks tap tap
Up and down the long green river
Ohe Ohe lanterns quiver
Willow branches brush the river
Ohe Ohe lanterns quiver
Waves lap lap
Fish fins clap clap
Brown sails flap flap
Chop-sticks tap tap

By Tao Lang Pee

I can join in with a poem.

1 Listen to your teacher read this poem two times then join in reading it.

Glossary

Ohe: a swinging, swaying sound
sampan: a flat bottomed Chinese boat
quiver: to shake quickly

Fishing boats

1 Answer these questions about the poem on page 94.
  a Find the words that are repeated in the poem.
  b Find four words that rhyme.
  c Find another two words that rhyme.
  d Are the words that rhyme spelt the same?

2 Here are some things you might find on a fishing boat, with a sound or action:
  • fishing line (squeak)
  • fishing boat (creak)
  • jumping fish (tumble)
  • my tummy (rumble).

Use the words to write your own poem:

Fishing boat sounds

Fishing line squeak squeak
Fishing boat _____ _____
Jumping _____ _____
My tummy _____ _____

What have I learnt?

In this unit, I have learnt to:
  • blend letters to help me read words
  • find words that rhyme
  • write my own poem
  • add actions to perform a poem.

QUIZ 2

1 Read the story.

Once upon a time, there was a boy called Pablo. One day Pablo was kind to an old man and the man gave him a goose. Pablo carried the goose home. On the way home a girl touched the goose and stuck to it. As Pablo walked more people stuck to the goose. Pablo walked past a castle. The princess saw Pablo walking with a line of people behind him. She laughed and fell in love with him. Pablo gave away the goose and married the princess.

a Who are the two main characters?

b What story words start the story?

c What happens at the end?
   i Pablo is kind to a man.
   ii People stick to Pablo.
   iii Pablo marries a princess.

d What happens in the middle?
   i Pablo is kind to a man.
   ii People stick to the goose.
   iii Pablo marries a princess.

2 Match the missing letters to the word:

| mp | lk | tr | nd |

a me__   **b** mi__   **c** __ip   **d** pu__

3 Match the part of a book to its description.

1. caption   2. heading   3. contents page

a A list of the topics in the book.
b A sentence that tells you about a picture.
c Words that tell you what the section below is about.

4 Use **and** to make one sentence for each pair.
a The ball went wide. The ball missed the goal.
b I bought an ice cream. I bought a comic.
c The girl has a red hat. The girl has a green coat.
d Sit on the carpet. Listen to me.
e The elephant drinks at the waterhole.
The zebra drinks at the waterhole.

5 Match the words that rhyme.

slip   lent   hold   stop   top   blot
bold   up   hot   trip   cup   bent

Unit 7 Fantasy stories

I can talk clearly about my thoughts.

I can talk about the books I like.

Looking at covers

Helpful hints

We learn about books from the cover.

WRITTEN BY IAN WHYBROW   ILLUSTRATED BY DAVID MELLING

Author – the person who wrote the book

Title – the name of the book

Picture – to give us a clue about the story

Illustrator – the person who drew the pictures

Blurb – this tells us about the story

Talk Partners

Look at a pile of storybooks in the classroom. With a partner talk about what might happen in each story. Look at:

• the picture • the blurb

Choose which book you want to read.

Tell your partner why.

I can read aloud from books on my own.

Reading stories

1 Read aloud the books you have chosen. Remember to:
- pause at the end of sentences
- use phonics to sound out words to read them.

2 Match the characters to their book.

a

b

c

d

e

f

I pause at the end of sentences.

The Tiger Who Came to Tea

Once there was a little girl called Sophie, and she was having tea with her mummy in the kitchen.

Suddenly there was a ring at the door.

Sophie opened the door, and there was a big, furry, stripy tiger. The tiger said, "Excuse me, but I'm very hungry. Do you think I could have tea with you?"

Sophie's mummy said, "Of course, come in."

1 Listen to your teacher read the story. Then read along with the story the next time. Pause at the end of sentences.

What happens next?

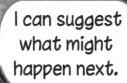

I can suggest what might happen next.

So the tiger came into the kitchen and sat down at the table.

Sophie's mummy said, "Would you like a sandwich?"

But the tiger didn't just take one sandwich. He took all the sandwiches on the plate and swallowed them in one big mouthful.

Owp!

And he still looked hungry, so Sophie passed him the buns.

From The Tiger Who Came to Tea by Judith Kerr

Talk Partners

Tell your partner what you think will happen next. Draw a picture and write a sentence underneath.

Did you know?

In *The Tiger Who Came to Tea* by Judith Kerr, the tiger eats all the food in the house and drinks all the water then leaves. Sophie and her parents go out to dinner and Sophie goes to bed without a bath.

Talking about a story

I can talk about what happens in a story.

1 Answer the questions about the story on pages 100–101.
  a Who are the three characters in the story?
     Hint: one is an animal.
  b What happens at the beginning?
  c What does Sophie say?
  d What does the tiger eat?

Talk Partners

Get into a group of three. Act out the story together. Act out the rest of the story using your ideas or the real end of the book.

2 Draw a picture of the tiger leaving at the end of the story. What will Sophie say to the tiger? Write it in a speech bubble.

Long ai and long ee

I know how to spell long vowel phonemes.

1 Find words in the story on pages 100–101.
  a Find two words with the ai phoneme spelt a_e.
  b Find one word with the ee phoneme spelt ea.
  c Find two words with the ee phoneme spelt y.

Helpful hints

The long ai phoneme is spelt:
• ai as in rain
• ay as in play
• a_e as in came
The long ee phoneme is spelt:
• ee as in feel
• ea as in tea
• e_e as in even
• y as in happy

2 Sort these words into two lists:
  a words with the ai phoneme
  b words with the ee phoneme.

neat   train   dotty   tray   eel
crate   tatty   tape   feet   sea
pail   cream   lane   these   stay
jolly   peep   rain

I can take part in a role play.

Who is coming to tea?

Talk Partners

Choose one of these characters to come to tea. Act out what happens with two friends.

Writing a simple story

I can write a simple storybook.

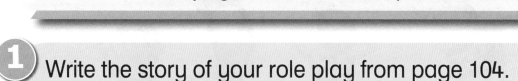

Talk Partners

Tell the story of your role play from page 104 to yourself. Tell the story to a partner. Tell the story again to a different partner.

1 Write the story of your role play from page 104.

  a Draw three pictures for the story:
   • The beginning – opening the door
   • The middle – what happens?
     What do you do with the character?
   • The end – the character goes.
  b Write one sentence underneath each picture.
  c Check your story using the checklist below.
  d Share your story with a new partner.
    Ask them to tell you what they think.

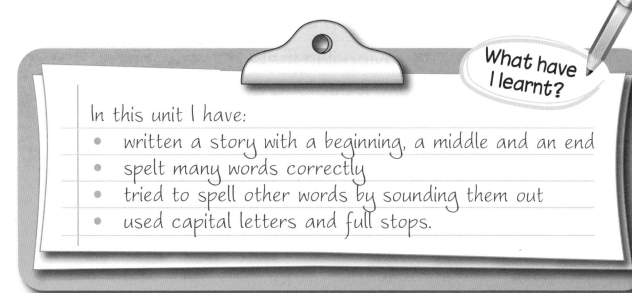

What have I learnt?

In this unit I have:
  • written a story with a beginning, a middle and an end
  • spelt many words correctly
  • tried to spell other words by sounding them out
  • used capital letters and full stops.

I can read some words on sight.

The Way Back Home

Once there was a boy and one day, as he was putting his things back in the cupboard, he found his aeroplane.

He didn't remember leaving it in there but he thought he'd take it out for a go straight away.

1 Read the story. Then practise reading and spelling these words.

back	in	what	for	but	he

The plane lifted off the ground and up and higher and higher and higher.

Suddenly his plane spluttered ... it had run out of petrol.

Now the boy was stuck on the moon. What was he to do?

From The Way Back Home by Oliver Jeffers

Glossary

spluttered: to make a pop-pop sound
petrol: a type of fuel

I can talk about the beginning, middle and end.

A good beginning

1 Answer these questions about the story on pages 106–107.
  a What happens at the beginning of the story?
  b Where does the boy go in his plane?
  c Is it really possible to go to the moon in a plane?

Talk Partners

What do you think will happen next?
What will happen to him on the moon?
What will happen at the end?
How will the boy get home in the end?

2 Write the word.

a

b

c

d

e

f

I can sound out words to spell them.

On the moon

Helpful hints

The **setting** is the place where a story takes place.
There can be more than one setting in a story.

1
a What is the first place the story is set in *The Way Back Home*?
b What do we see there?
Choose two.

> a cupboard   a plane   toys
> stars   the moon

2
a Where does the boy go in his plane?
b What do we see there? Choose two.

> a cupboard   stars   a plane   toys   the moon

3 Look at these settings. Talk about them with a partner.
Write a caption for each one.

a

b

Retelling a story

I can retell a story.

Did you know?

In the story, an alien crash lands on the moon. He gives the boy some petrol. The boy flies home. He picks up some tools and returns to the moon. He fixes the alien's spaceship. They say goodbye.

Talk Partners

Use these pictures to tell the story of *The Way Back Home* with a partner. Take turns to tell it to each other.

a

boy

aeroplane

b

moon

no petrol

c

alien

spaceship

d

e

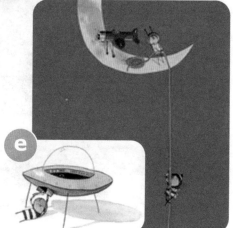

Writing sentences

I can write sentences to retell a story.

1

Look at the pictures on page 110. Write a sentence for each picture. Hint: to write words, say each word slowly and listen to the different sounds (phonemes). Write the letters for the phoneme. Remember: you might need two letters for one phoneme.

Helpful hints

The long **oo** phoneme can be spelt:
- **oo** as in m**oo**n
- **ew** as in f**ew**
- **u_e** as in h**u**g**e**

2

Complete the words:

a fl _ t _

b scr _ _

c sp _ _ n

d t _ b _

e t _ _ th

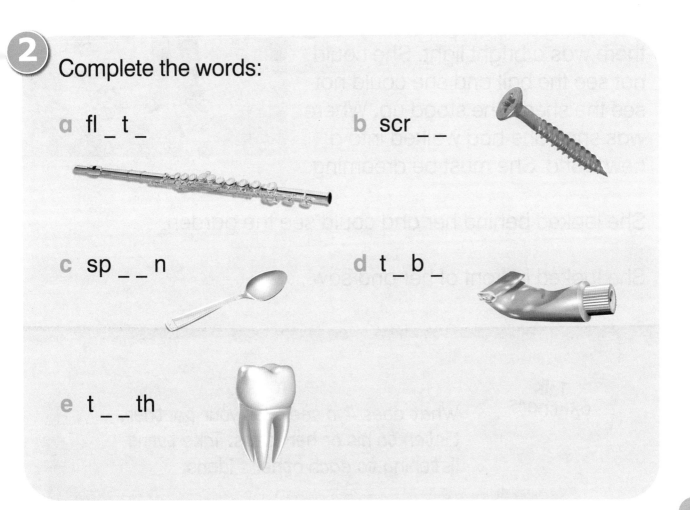

Ayo's surprise

I can take turns when speaking.

1 Read this story opener.

Once upon a time there was a girl called Ayo.

One day she was playing with her ball in the garden when it rolled behind the shed. She squeezed behind the shed to get it. Suddenly there was a bright light. She could not see the ball and she could not see the shed. She stood up. Where was she? She had walked into a new world. She must be dreaming.

She looked behind her and could see the garden.

She looked in front of her and saw ...

Talk Partners

What does Ayo see? Tell your partner. Listen to his or her ideas. Take turns listening to each other's ideas.

I can take part in a role play.

Through the gap

1 Where do you think the space behind the shed takes Ayo? Choose one of these settings and act it out with a partner.

a She goes back to the time of dinosaurs.

b She turns into a secret agent.

c She finds herself in space.

d She finds a castle in the desert.

I can use the word **and**.

What happened next?

1 Look at the pictures on page 113. Write an ending for each of these sentences.

a Ayo saw the dinosaur and _____.
b Ayo saw the man with the bag and _____.
c Ayo landed her spaceship and _____.
d There was a girl in front of a castle and _____.

2 Draw four pictures to tell a story about Ayo.

a Beginning: Picture 1 – Ayo going to get her ball.
b Middle: Picture 2 – Ayo arriving in a new world.
c Middle: Picture 3 – Ayo doing something in the new world.
d End: Picture 4 – Ayo arriving home.

3 Write a sentence under each picture. Try to use **and** in one sentence.

I can read and talk about my own writing.

I can use story language.

Once upon a time

1 Find these words in the story starter on page 112.
- Once upon a time
- One day
- Suddenly

2 Add one of these to your story:
a Beginning words: Once upon a time, One day
b Middle: next, suddenly
c End: at last, in the end

3 Share your story with a friend. Tell him or her about it. Ask him or her to tell you what they like and what you should change.

What have I learnt?

In this unit I have:
- learnt what is on the cover of a storybook
- thought about what might happen next in a story
- written a story with a beginning, a middle and an end
- written sentences with a capital letter and a full stop
- written a sentence using the word and
- made my story better by sharing it with a friend.

Recounts

Recount

I know that some texts look different.

Helpful hints

A **recount** is a true story of something that happened. It could be:

- a school trip
- something funny that happened
- something exciting that happened.

Recounts told by the person in the story will have sentences with **I** or **we** in them.

- **I** went to the shops.
- **We** fell down a hole.

1 Read these recounts.

a   b   c

When I was six I became a pirate in a play.

On Monday, our class went to the farm.

Last week, I went to a party as an astronaut.

Making links

I can make a connection with my own life.

1 Read these recounts. Tell your partner when something similar happened to you.

a Last week, my mother took me to the dentist. I felt scared when we were waiting.

b I worked hard in maths. The teacher gave me a gold star. I was so pleased I went bright pink.

c At last we set off on holiday. When we had driven for five minutes, my sister said she had forgotten her teddy. Dad was cross.

d Yesterday, we went to my auntie's wedding. It was fun to begin with. We danced and ate cake. But it went on and on. I fell asleep under a table.

117

I can talk about the books I like.

Stuck in the ice

An icy adventure
My name is Sir Ernest Shackleton. Many years ago I tried to go to the South Pole.

Trapped in the ice
When we were on the way to the South Pole, our ship became stuck in the ice. We lived on the ship all winter. It was dark most of the time. We sang songs and played games.

We played football on the ice.

Talk Partners

Listen to your teacher read this recount then read it with a partner. Talk about what makes the story interesting.

I can read some words on sight.

The ship sinks

In the end the ship sank into the ice. For half a year we pulled our lifeboats across the ice, eating seals to stay alive. When we reached the sea, we climbed into our lifeboats.

Elephant Island

We found a small empty island called Elephant Island. Most of the men stayed there. Five of us sailed off to find an island with some people on. It took many weeks but I came back with a new boat and everyone was rescued.

On Elephant Island the men made a house from a boat.

1 Find these words in the recount above and practise reading and writing them.

were   into   called

house   made   people

Word endings

I can talk about what happens in a story.

1 Tell your teacher the answers to these questions.

a Who is telling this recount?
This recount is told by _____.

b Where did he want to go?
He wanted to go to _____.

c What happened to the ship?
The ship _____.

d What was the name of the island they found?
The island was called _____.

e Is the story true or false?
It is _____.

Helpful hints

Some words end in –ing, –ed or –s.

–ing words
- walking = walk + ing
- raining = rain + ing

–ed words
- walked = walk + ed
- rained = rain + ed

–s words
- walks = walk + s
- rains = rain + s

Adding –ed, –ing and –s

I know some common word endings.

1 Find these words in the recount on pages 118–119. Split them into root words and endings. The first one has been done for you. The Helpful hints box on page 120 will help you.

a pulled = pull + ed
b played
c climbed
d sailed

e eating
f weeks
g songs

2 Add –s, –ing or –ed to finish the words.

a egg _

b jump _ _ _

c kick _ _

d sing _

I can share an experience.

I can listen to others and ask questions.

My day out

Talk Partners

Tell your partner about an event or outing you went on with your family.
Use this frame to talk about it:

One day, I went to _____
I saw _____
We ate _____
At the end of the day we _____

Talk Partners

Listen to your partner's story.
Ask them questions about it.

Talk Partners

Show your partner that you listened to their story by telling it back to them.

I can recount an event.

Writing my recount

1 Write your recount

a Take a piece of paper.
Fold it into four sections.

b Write these sentence starters in each section.

One day, I went to_____.
I saw_____.
We ate_____.
At the end of the day we_____.

c Complete the sentences for your family trip.

d Draw a picture for each section.

One day, I went to a park.	

2 Share your recount with a partner. Listen to their recount.
Check both recounts:

• Have you used capital letters and full stops?
• Have you spelt most words right?

Write a second sentence for each section. For example:

We _____ there.

First we _____.

Next we _____.

We felt _____.

Try this

123

The school trip

I can talk clearly.

Last Friday we went on a school trip to a lake.

It was very hot on the coach, but when we reached the lake, we put our hands in the cool water. It was bliss.

1 Read the recount. Tell your partner what happened. Remember to talk clearly so that your partner can hear you.

We went by boat across the lake. I put my hand in the water and watched the sun sparkle on the water drops.

We had our lunch on the other side of the lake. There were some ducks that wanted lunch too. We let them have our leftover food.

We all slept on the coach on the way home.

2

Can you find words with long phonemes?
a Find one word with the long **ai** spelt **a_e.**
b Find one word with the long **ai** spelt **ay.**
c Write these words in two columns as shown below:

> cake   play   fake   stay   pale   name
> day   tray   plane   clay

spelt **ay**	spelt **a_e**
clay	name

Cool, fool and tool

I know how to spell long vowel phonemes.

1 Answer 'true' or 'false'.
a It was cool on the coach.
b It was hot at the lake.
c The ducks ate the lunch.
d The recount is an instruction.
e The light made patterns on the water.

2 Find **oa** and **oo** words on pages 124–125.
a Find one word with the long **oa** phoneme spelt **oa**.
b Find one word with the long **oa** phoneme spelt **o_e**.
c Find one word with the long **oo** phoneme spelt **oo**.

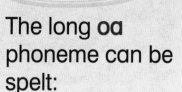

Helpful hints

The long **oa** phoneme can be spelt:
• **oa** as in coat
• **o_e** as in pole
• **ow** as in snow.
The long **oo** phoneme can be spelt:
• **oo** as in tool
• **u_e** as in huge
• **ew** as in new.

Spelling words

I can spell many familiar words.

1

Look at these words. Put them into two lists:

a words with the **oa** phoneme
b words with the **oo** phoneme.

oa words	oo words
blow	tune

boat   coach   float   flown   grow   home
stove   hope   flow   cool   school   coat
pool   tool   balloon   huge   tune
newt   flute   grew   stew   hoop

2

Look at these pictures. Write a word for each one.

a   sp_ _ _

b   sn_ _

c   o_ _ _

d   m_ _ _

e   bl_ _

f   b_ _ _

I can use a full stop.

I can use the word **and.**

Practising sentences

Helpful hints

Remember!
When we write a **sentence** we *must:*
- use a capital letter for the first word
- use a capital letter for the word **I**
- put a full stop at the end.

When we write a sentence we *can:*
- use **and** to say more than one thing.

1 The words in these sentences are muddled up. Put the words in the right order to write the sentence. You will need to add a capital letter and a full stop.

a ate lunch the lake and we went to

b we had an took my sister me to the park ice cream and

c went inside the door I opened and

2 Write a sentence for each picture.

a

b

I can talk clearly about my thoughts.

I can take turns when speaking.

Do you remember?

Talk Partners

With a partner, talk about a school trip you have been on. Remember to:
- Talk clearly so your partner can hear you.
- Take turns speaking.
- Listen to what your partner has to say.

Helpful hints

Here are some useful words for telling a **recount**:
- One day
- At first
- Next
- Then
- Suddenly
- We had fun
- In the end
- Finally

1 Say some sentences about your trip. Use these starters:
a One day we went to _____.
b We went on _____.
c First we _____.
d Then we _____.
e Finally we _____.

I can use the right words.

I can write sentences to tell a recount.

Our trip

1 Take a long strip of paper and use it to make a zigzag book.
Draw five pictures to tell the story of your class trip.

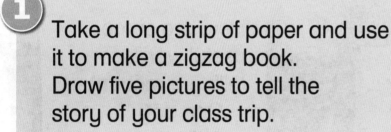

My visit to the Aquarium

2 Use your zigzag book to tell the story of your trip to yourself or to a partner.

a Use some of the useful words from page 129.

b Use some words to do with the trip, for example:
- museum
- park
- wildlife centre.

3 Write a sentence under each picture.
Remember to use the words you've practised.

Sharing work

I can read and talk about my own writing.

1 Check your story. Read it to yourself. Use the checklist at the bottom of this page.

2 Share your story with a partner.

a Ask your partner what they like. Ask him or her to help you make it better.

b Read your partner's story. Tell him or her what you like.

c Talk with your partner about how the recounts are the same and how they are different.

What have I learnt?

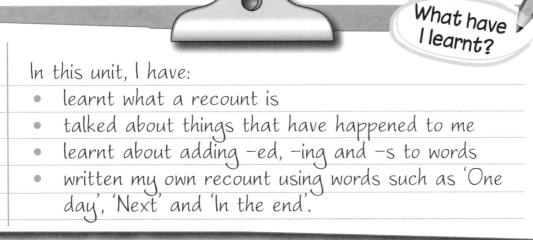

In this unit, I have:
- learnt what a recount is
- talked about things that have happened to me
- learnt about adding –ed, –ing and –s to words
- written my own recount using words such as 'One day', 'Next' and 'In the end'.

Animal poems

I can use phonics to read words I don't know.

I can read along with a poem.

Chimpanzee

It's great to be a chimpanzee
Swinging through the trees
And if we can't find nuts to eat
We munch each other's fleas!

By Giles Andreae

1 Listen to your teacher read the poem. Join in a second time. Point to each word as you read.

2 Break these words into phonemes to read them:

ch–i–m–p–a–n–z–ee

s–w–i–ng–i–ng

 **Did you know?**

Chimpanzees spend hours every day cleaning each other's hair and removing fleas.

Rhyming words

I can look at the spelling patterns in words that rhyme.

1 Answer the questions about the poem on page 132.
  a How do the chimpanzees move?
  b What two things do they like to eat?
  c How do they eat fleas?

2 Rhyming ee
  a Write the six words in the 'Chimpanzee' poem with a long ee phoneme.
  b Which words rhyme? Underline the parts of the words that sound the same.
  c Choose words from the cloud that rhyme with **trees**. Underline the parts of the words that rhyme.

> feet   ice   beat   bees   knees   breeze   size

  d Choose words from the cloud that rhyme with **eat**. Underline the parts of the words that rhyme.

Jungle animals

I can recite a poem.

1 Can you learn the 'Chimpanzee' poem by heart?

a Listen to your teacher read the poem.

b Join in reading it.

c Try to read it on your own.

d Spot the rhymes.

e Can you remember lines two and four?

  1. It's great to be a chimpanzee

  2. _____

  3. And if we can't find nuts to eat

  4. _____

f Practise remembering lines one and three:

  1. _____

  2. Swinging through the trees

  3. _____

  4. We munch each other's fleas!

Jungle poem

I can write a new verse.

1 Pair up the words that rhyme.

sun   leaves   pool   run   cool   trees

2 Use the words in the cloud above to complete this poem.

It's great to be an elephant
Munching at the _____
And if I can't quite reach them
I just knock down the _____

It's great to be a lion
Sleeping in the _____
When I wake, I give a roar
And watch the zebra _____

It's great to be a hippo
Bathing in a _____
Even in the hot, hot sun
It keeps me very _____

Mice

I think mice
are rather nice.

Their tails are long,
Their faces small,
They haven't any
Chins at all.

Their ears are pink,
Their teeth are white,
They run about
The house at night.

They nibble things
They shouldn't touch
And no one seems
To like them much.

But I think mice
Are nice

By Rose Fyleman

Liking mice

I can spot words ending in **s.**

1 Write all the words in the poem on page 136 that end in **–s.**

Helpful hints

We add **s** to say there is more than one.
1 thing – 2 things
1 face – 2 faces

2 Write the word.

a one _____

b two _____

c one _____

d four _____

e one _____

f three _____

Finding patterns

I can talk about the words in a poem.

1 Find the word in the poem on page 136 that rhymes with:
a small _____
b white _____
c touch _____
d mice _____

2 Look at the words in the poem.
a Find the words 'I think mice are nice' two times in the poem.
b Find the lines beginning 'Their'. What do the mice look like?
c Find the lines beginning 'They'. What do the mice do?

Talk Partners

Read the poem with a partner. Tell your partner what you like about the poem.

I can read
long vowels.

Long vowels

1 Find words in the poem on page 136:
   a Two words with a long ee phoneme, spelt ee.
   b Two words with the long igh phoneme spelt i_e.
   c One word with the long igh phoneme spelt igh.
   d One word with the long ai phoneme spelt ai.
   e One word with the long ai phoneme spelt a_e.

2 Find phonemes in the words in the cloud below.
Practise spelling the words.

> like   I   day   make   no
>   see   time   we   too

Snake in school

One year in the Monsoon season
We all screamed and with good reason:
A water snake had come to school!
But Mister Singh just kept his cool.
He chased him out of our school gate
And told him off for being late!

By Debjani Chatterjee

1 Listen to your teacher read 'Snake in school', then join in a second time. Read 'Snake in school' aloud. Use a clear voice.

Glossary

Monsoon: winds that bring heavy rains to hot countries

I know that we talk in different ways.

I can use the right words.

Different types of talk

1 Draw a picture to go with the 'Snake in school' poem.
Write a sentence about the snake under the picture.
Use these words from the poem.

> snake   school   chased   gate

Talk Partners We sometimes talk in different ways. Talk to your partner about how these people talk.

a Two friends talking.

b Reading a poem aloud in class.

c Saying sorry to your mother.

2 Practise reading the poem on page 140 with a partner.
Read it out loud together to the rest of the class.

1 Read this story.

Once upon a time there were two friends called Bert and Ernie. Bert was a very shy shark and Ernie was a very brave fish. They lived together in a coral reef.

a Is this the beginning, middle or end of the story?

b Who are the two characters?

c Where is the story set?

2 Use the words in the cloud below to create a phonemes table like this one:

ai	ee	igh	oa	oo
play	feet	fly	boat	moon
rain	cream	high	slow	flute
tape		kite	pole	

> pain   beat   plate   hole
> seem   plain   bite   snow   float
> flight   tune   cry   pool

3 Read the text.

The day we went to the seaside it was wet and windy. We could not have our picnic or make a sandcastle. The waves were huge so we jumped and splashed in the waves. It was great but very cold. Afterwards, we went to the cafe and drank hot chocolate.

Answer the questions.
a Where did they go?
b What could they not do?
c What did they do?
d What sort of text is it?
   poem   instruction   recount

4 Add –**ing**, –**ed** or –**s** to these words. You can use each ending only once.

a fly _____   b pack _____   c girl _____

5 Write a sentence to go with each picture. Use **and**.

a

b

6 Complete the words.

a   _ c _ cr _ _ m

b   sk _ t _ _ _

c   scr _ _

d   n _ _ _ t